The prayer MAP

for

COURAGEOUS

Girls

A CREATIVE
JOURNAL

SHILOH ! kidz
An Imprint of Barbour Publishing, Inc.

Published by Shiloh Kidz, an imprint of Barbour Publishing, Inc., 1810 Barbour Drive, Uhrichsville, Ohio 44683, www.shilohkidz.com

Our mission is to inspire the world with the life-changing message of the Bible.

Member of the
Evangelical Christian
Publishers Association

Printed in China.

06651 1019 DS

EVEN THOUGH I AM A COURAGEOUS GIRL, I SOMETIMES WORRY ABOUT THINGS. RIGHT NOW I AM WORRIED ABOUT. . .

AREAS OF MY LIFE WHERE I COULD USE SOME EXTRA COURAGE INCLUDE. . .

The life of a courageous girl is quite busy. Here's what's going on in my life that I need to share with You, God. . .

THANK YOU, GOD, FOR MAKING ME A COURAGEOUS GIRL!

Thank You, God, for hearing my prayers! AMEN.

I am sure that God Who began the good work in you will keep on working in you until the day Jesus Christ comes again.

PHILIPPIANS 1:6

YOU GIVE ME COURAGE JUST WHEN I NEED IT THE MOST. AND I AM SO THANKFUL! I AM ALSO THANKFUL FOR. . .

You forgive me when I make mistakes—whether they're super small or SUPER BIG. Today, I need Your forgiveness for. . .

I want to shine my light for You, God, so others can see it. And I would like to help build up courage in others too. People I am praying for today. . .

EVEN THOUGH I AM A COURAGEOUS GIRL, I SOMETIMES WORRY ABOUT THINGS. RIGHT NOW I AM WORRIED ABOUT. . .

AREAS OF MY LIFE WHERE I COULD USE SOME EXTRA COURAGE INCLUDE. . .

The life of a courageous girl is quite busy. Here's what's going on in my life that I need to share with You, God. . .

THANK YOU, GOD, FOR MAKING ME A COURAGEOUS GIRL!

Thank You, God, for hearing my prayers! AMEN.

I do everything to spread the Good News and share in its blessings.

1 CORINTHIANS 9:23 NLT

DATE:

Dear God...

YOU GIVE ME COURAGE JUST WHEN I NEED IT THE MOST. AND I AM SO THANKFUL! I AM ALSO THANKFUL FOR. . .

You forgive me when I make mistakes—whether they're super small or SUPER BIG. Today, I need Your forgiveness for. . .

I want to shine my light for You, God, so others can see it. And I would like to help build up courage in others too. People I am praying for today. . .

EVEN THOUGH I AM A COURAGEOUS GIRL, I SOMETIMES WORRY ABOUT THINGS. RIGHT NOW I AM WORRIED ABOUT. . .

....

....

....

AREAS OF MY LIFE WHERE I COULD USE SOME EXTRA COURAGE INCLUDE. . .

The life of a courageous girl is quite busy. Here's what's going on in my life that I need to share with You, God. . .

....

....

....

....

....

....

....

....

....

THANK YOU, GOD, FOR MAKING ME A COURAGEOUS GIRL!

Thank You, God, for hearing my prayers! AMEN.

Whatever work you do, do it with all your heart.

COLOSSIANS 3:23

DATE: Dear God. . .

YOU GIVE ME COURAGE JUST WHEN I NEED IT THE MOST. AND I AM SO
THANKFUL! I AM ALSO THANKFUL FOR. . .

You forgive me when I make
mistakes—whether they're super
small or SUPER BIG. Today, I need
Your forgiveness for. . .

I want to shine my light for
You, God, so others can
see it. And I would like to
help build up courage in
others too. People I am
praying for today. . .

EVEN THOUGH I AM A COURAGEOUS GIRL, I SOMETIMES
WORRY ABOUT THINGS. RIGHT NOW I AM WORRIED ABOUT. . .

....
....
....
....

AREAS OF MY LIFE WHERE I COULD USE SOME
EXTRA COURAGE INCLUDE. . .

....
....
....
....
....
....
....

The life of a courageous girl
is quite busy. Here's what's
going on in my life that I need
to share with You, God. . .

....
....
....
....
....
....
....
....

THANK YOU, GOD, FOR MAKING ME A
COURAGEOUS GIRL!

Thank You, God,
for hearing my prayers!
AMEN.

Stand firm in the faith.
Be courageous. Be strong.

1 CORINTHIANS 16:13 NLT

Dear God. . .

YOU GIVE ME COURAGE JUST WHEN I NEED IT THE MOST. AND I AM SO
THANKFUL! I AM ALSO THANKFUL FOR. . .

You forgive me when I make
mistakes—whether they're super
small or SUPER BIG. Today, I need
Your forgiveness for. . .

I want to shine my light for
You, God, so others can
see it. And I would like to
help build up courage in
others too. People I am
praying for today. . .

EVEN THOUGH I AM A COURAGEOUS GIRL, I SOMETIMES
WORRY ABOUT THINGS. RIGHT NOW I AM WORRIED ABOUT. . .

....

....

....

....

AREAS OF MY LIFE WHERE I COULD USE SOME
EXTRA COURAGE INCLUDE. . .

The life of a courageous girl
is quite busy. Here's what's
going on in my life that I need
to share with You, God. . .

....

....

....

....

....

....

....

....

THANK YOU, GOD, FOR MAKING ME A
COURAGEOUS GIRL!

Thank You, God,
for hearing my prayers!
AMEN.

*"[God] makes known secret
and hidden things."*

DANIEL 2:22

YOU GIVE ME COURAGE JUST WHEN I NEED IT THE MOST. AND I AM SO
THANKFUL! I AM ALSO THANKFUL FOR. . .

You forgive me when I make
mistakes—whether they're super
small or SUPER BIG. Today, I need
Your forgiveness for. . .

I want to shine my light for
You, God, so others can
see it. And I would like to
help build up courage in
others too. People I am
praying for today. . .

EVEN THOUGH I AM A COURAGEOUS GIRL, I SOMETIMES
WORRY ABOUT THINGS. RIGHT NOW I AM WORRIED ABOUT. . .

....

....

....

....

AREAS OF MY LIFE WHERE I COULD USE SOME
EXTRA COURAGE INCLUDE. . .

The life of a courageous girl
is quite busy. Here's what's
going on in my life that I need
to share with You, God. . .

THANK YOU, GOD, FOR MAKING ME A
COURAGEOUS GIRL!

Thank You, God,
for hearing my prayers!
AMEN.

*I will lift up my eyes to the mountains. Where
will my help come from? My help comes from
the Lord, Who made heaven and earth.*

PSALM 121:1-2

YOU GIVE ME COURAGE JUST WHEN I NEED IT THE MOST. AND I AM SO THANKFUL! I AM ALSO THANKFUL FOR. . .

You forgive me when I make mistakes—whether they're super small or SUPER BIG. Today, I need Your forgiveness for. . .

I want to shine my light for You, God, so others can see it. And I would like to help build up courage in others too. People I am praying for today. . .

EVEN THOUGH I AM A COURAGEOUS GIRL, I SOMETIMES
WORRY ABOUT THINGS. RIGHT NOW I AM WORRIED ABOUT. . .

....

....

....

....

AREAS OF MY LIFE WHERE I COULD USE SOME
EXTRA COURAGE INCLUDE. . .

....

....

....

....

....

....

....

The life of a courageous girl
is quite busy. Here's what's
going on in my life that I need
to share with You, God. . .

....

....

....

....

....

....

....

....

THANK YOU, GOD, FOR MAKING ME A
COURAGEOUS GIRL!

Thank You, God,
for hearing my prayers!
AMEN.

*For God did not give us a spirit of fear.
He gave us a spirit of power and of
love and of a good mind.*

2 TIMOTHY 1:7

YOU GIVE ME COURAGE JUST WHEN I NEED IT THE MOST. AND I AM SO
THANKFUL! I AM ALSO THANKFUL FOR. . .

You forgive me when I make
mistakes—whether they're super
small or SUPER BIG. Today, I need
Your forgiveness for. . .

I want to shine my light for
You, God, so others can
see it. And I would like to
help build up courage in
others too. People I am
praying for today. . .

EVEN THOUGH I AM A COURAGEOUS GIRL, I SOMETIMES WORRY ABOUT THINGS. RIGHT NOW I AM WORRIED ABOUT. . .

....

....

....

....

AREAS OF MY LIFE WHERE I COULD USE SOME EXTRA COURAGE INCLUDE. . .

....

....

....

....

....

....

....

The life of a courageous girl is quite busy. Here's what's going on in my life that I need to share with You, God. . .

....

....

....

....

....

....

....

....

THANK YOU, GOD, FOR MAKING ME A COURAGEOUS GIRL!

Thank You, God, for hearing my prayers! AMEN.

Let no one show little respect for you because you are young. Show other Christians how to live by your life. They should be able to follow you in the way you talk and in what you do. Show them how to live in faith and in love and in holy living.

1 TIMOTHY 4:12

YOU GIVE ME COURAGE JUST WHEN I NEED IT THE MOST. AND I AM SO THANKFUL! I AM ALSO THANKFUL FOR. . .

You forgive me when I make mistakes—whether they're super small or SUPER BIG. Today, I need Your forgiveness for. . .

I want to shine my light for You, God, so others can see it. And I would like to help build up courage in others too. People I am praying for today. . .

EVEN THOUGH I AM A COURAGEOUS GIRL, I SOMETIMES
WORRY ABOUT THINGS. RIGHT NOW I AM WORRIED ABOUT. . .

....
....
....
....

AREAS OF MY LIFE WHERE I COULD USE SOME
EXTRA COURAGE INCLUDE. . .

....
....
....
....
....
....
....

The life of a courageous girl
is quite busy. Here's what's
going on in my life that I need
to share with You, God. . .

....
....
....
....
....
....
....

THANK YOU, GOD, FOR MAKING ME A
COURAGEOUS GIRL!

Thank You, God,
for hearing my prayers!
AMEN.

*Honor and thanks be to the Lord,
Who carries our heavy loads day by day.
He is the God Who saves us. Our God
is a God Who sets us free.*

PSALM 68:19–20

Dear God. . .

YOU GIVE ME COURAGE JUST WHEN I NEED IT THE MOST. AND I AM SO
THANKFUL! I AM ALSO THANKFUL FOR. . . ..

....

....

....

....

You forgive me when I make
mistakes—whether they're super
small or SUPER BIG. Today, I need
Your forgiveness for. . .

I want to shine my light for
You, God, so others can
see it. And I would like to
help build up courage in
others too. People I am
praying for today. . .

EVEN THOUGH I AM A COURAGEOUS GIRL, I SOMETIMES WORRY ABOUT THINGS. RIGHT NOW I AM WORRIED ABOUT. . .

....

....

....

AREAS OF MY LIFE WHERE I COULD USE SOME EXTRA COURAGE INCLUDE. . .

....

....

....

....

....

....

The life of a courageous girl is quite busy. Here's what's going on in my life that I need to share with You, God. . .

....

....

....

....

....

....

....

THANK YOU, GOD, FOR MAKING ME A COURAGEOUS GIRL!

Thank You, God, for hearing my prayers! AMEN.

When I am afraid, I will trust you. I praise God for his word. I trust God, so I am not afraid. What can human beings do to me?

PSALM 56:3–4 NCV

YOU GIVE ME COURAGE JUST WHEN I NEED IT THE MOST. AND I AM SO
THANKFUL! I AM ALSO THANKFUL FOR. . .

You forgive me when I make
mistakes—whether they're super
small or SUPER BIG. Today, I need
Your forgiveness for. . .

I want to shine my light for
You, God, so others can
see it. And I would like to
help build up courage in
others too. People I am
praying for today. . .

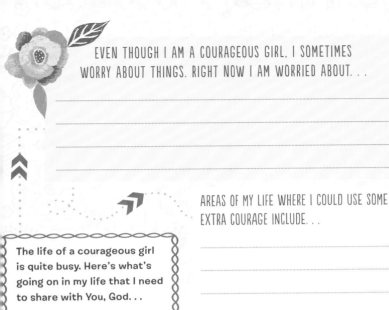

EVEN THOUGH I AM A COURAGEOUS GIRL, I SOMETIMES WORRY ABOUT THINGS. RIGHT NOW I AM WORRIED ABOUT...

....
....
....
....

AREAS OF MY LIFE WHERE I COULD USE SOME EXTRA COURAGE INCLUDE...

....
....
....
....
....
....
....

The life of a courageous girl is quite busy. Here's what's going on in my life that I need to share with You, God...

....
....
....
....
....
....
....
....

THANK YOU, GOD, FOR MAKING ME A COURAGEOUS GIRL!

Thank You, God, for hearing my prayers! AMEN.

"I can see, for sure, that God does not respect one person more than another."

ACTS 10:34

YOU GIVE ME COURAGE JUST WHEN I NEED IT THE MOST. AND I AM SO THANKFUL! I AM ALSO THANKFUL FOR. . .

You forgive me when I make mistakes—whether they're super small or SUPER BIG. Today, I need Your forgiveness for. . .

I want to shine my light for You, God, so others can see it. And I would like to help build up courage in others too. People I am praying for today. . .

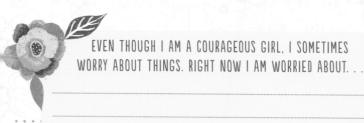

EVEN THOUGH I AM A COURAGEOUS GIRL, I SOMETIMES WORRY ABOUT THINGS. RIGHT NOW I AM WORRIED ABOUT. . .

AREAS OF MY LIFE WHERE I COULD USE SOME EXTRA COURAGE INCLUDE. . .

The life of a courageous girl is quite busy. Here's what's going on in my life that I need to share with You, God. . .

THANK YOU, GOD, FOR MAKING ME A COURAGEOUS GIRL!

Thank You, God, for hearing my prayers!
AMEN.

I can do all things because Christ gives me the strength.

PHILIPPIANS 4:13

DATE: Dear God. . .

YOU GIVE ME COURAGE JUST WHEN I NEED IT THE MOST. AND I AM SO THANKFUL! I AM ALSO THANKFUL FOR. . .

You forgive me when I make mistakes—whether they're super small or SUPER BIG. Today, I need Your forgiveness for. . .

I want to shine my light for You, God, so others can see it. And I would like to help build up courage in others too. People I am praying for today. . .

EVEN THOUGH I AM A COURAGEOUS GIRL, I SOMETIMES WORRY ABOUT THINGS. RIGHT NOW I AM WORRIED ABOUT. . .

....
....
....
....

AREAS OF MY LIFE WHERE I COULD USE SOME EXTRA COURAGE INCLUDE. . .

....
....
....
....
....
....
....

The life of a courageous girl is quite busy. Here's what's going on in my life that I need to share with You, God. . .

....
....
....
....
....
....
....

THANK YOU, GOD, FOR MAKING ME A COURAGEOUS GIRL!

Thank You, God, for hearing my prayers! AMEN.

A friend loves you all the time.

PROVERBS 17:17 NCV

YOU GIVE ME COURAGE JUST WHEN I NEED IT THE MOST. AND I AM SO
THANKFUL! I AM ALSO THANKFUL FOR. . .

You forgive me when I make
mistakes—whether they're super
small or SUPER BIG. Today, I need
Your forgiveness for. . .

I want to shine my light for
You, God, so others can
see it. And I would like to
help build up courage in
others too. People I am
praying for today. . .

EVEN THOUGH I AM A COURAGEOUS GIRL, I SOMETIMES WORRY ABOUT THINGS. RIGHT NOW I AM WORRIED ABOUT. . .

....

....

....

....

AREAS OF MY LIFE WHERE I COULD USE SOME EXTRA COURAGE INCLUDE. . .

....

....

....

....

....

....

The life of a courageous girl is quite busy. Here's what's going on in my life that I need to share with You, God. . .

....

....

....

....

....

....

....

....

....

THANK YOU, GOD, FOR MAKING ME A COURAGEOUS GIRL!

Thank You, God, for hearing my prayers! AMEN.

But how can they call on Him if they have not put their trust in Him? And how can they put their trust in Him if they have not heard of Him? And how can they hear of Him unless someone tells them?

ROMANS 10:14

YOU GIVE ME COURAGE JUST WHEN I NEED IT THE MOST. AND I AM SO
THANKFUL! I AM ALSO THANKFUL FOR. . .

You forgive me when I make
mistakes—whether they're super
small or SUPER BIG. Today, I need
Your forgiveness for. . .

I want to shine my light for
You, God, so others can
see it. And I would like to
help build up courage in
others too. People I am
praying for today. . .

EVEN THOUGH I AM A COURAGEOUS GIRL, I SOMETIMES
WORRY ABOUT THINGS. RIGHT NOW I AM WORRIED ABOUT. . .

....

....

....

....

AREAS OF MY LIFE WHERE I COULD USE SOME
EXTRA COURAGE INCLUDE. . .

....

....

The life of a courageous girl
is quite busy. Here's what's
going on in my life that I need
to share with You, God. . .

....

....

....

....

....

....

....

....

....

THANK YOU, GOD, FOR MAKING ME A
COURAGEOUS GIRL!

**Thank You, God,
for hearing my prayers!
AMEN.**

*"I tell you, My Father in heaven does not want
one of these little children to be lost."*

MATTHEW 18:14

DATE: _____

Dear God. . .

YOU GIVE ME COURAGE JUST WHEN I NEED IT THE MOST. AND I AM SO THANKFUL! I AM ALSO THANKFUL FOR. . .

....

....

....

....

You forgive me when I make mistakes—whether they're super small or SUPER BIG. Today, I need Your forgiveness for. . .

....

....

....

....

....

....

....

....

....

....

I want to shine my light for You, God, so others can see it. And I would like to help build up courage in others too. People I am praying for today. . .

....

....

....

....

....

....

....

....

....

....

....

EVEN THOUGH I AM A COURAGEOUS GIRL, I SOMETIMES
WORRY ABOUT THINGS. RIGHT NOW I AM WORRIED ABOUT. . .

....

....

....

....

AREAS OF MY LIFE WHERE I COULD USE SOME
EXTRA COURAGE INCLUDE. . .

....

....

....

....

....

....

....

The life of a courageous girl
is quite busy. Here's what's
going on in my life that I need
to share with You, God. . .

....

....

....

....

....

....

....

THANK YOU, GOD, FOR MAKING ME A
COURAGEOUS GIRL!

Thank You, God,
for hearing my prayers!
AMEN.

*A glad heart is good medicine, but a broken
spirit dries up the bones.*

PROVERBS 17:22

DATE: _____

Dear God. . . ➤➤

YOU GIVE ME COURAGE JUST WHEN I NEED IT THE MOST. AND I AM SO
THANKFUL! I AM ALSO THANKFUL FOR. . . ..
....
....
....
....

You forgive me when I make
mistakes—whether they're super
small or SUPER BIG. Today, I need
Your forgiveness for. . .

....
....
....
....
....
....
....
....
....
....
....

I want to shine my light for
You, God, so others can
see it. And I would like to
help build up courage in
others too. People I am
praying for today. . .

....
....
....
....
....
....
....
....
....
....
....
....
....

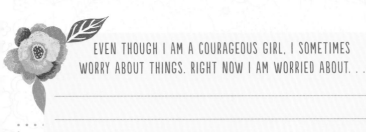

EVEN THOUGH I AM A COURAGEOUS GIRL, I SOMETIMES WORRY ABOUT THINGS. RIGHT NOW I AM WORRIED ABOUT. . .

....
....
....
....

AREAS OF MY LIFE WHERE I COULD USE SOME EXTRA COURAGE INCLUDE. . .

....
....
....
....
....
....
....

The life of a courageous girl is quite busy. Here's what's going on in my life that I need to share with You, God. . .

....
....
....
....
....
....
....
....

THANK YOU, GOD, FOR MAKING ME A COURAGEOUS GIRL!

Thank You, God, for hearing my prayers! AMEN.

"Be strong and courageous, and do the work. Don't be afraid or discouraged, for the LORD God, my God, is with you."

1 CHRONICLES 28:20 NLT

YOU GIVE ME COURAGE JUST WHEN I NEED IT THE MOST. AND I AM SO THANKFUL! I AM ALSO THANKFUL FOR. . .

You forgive me when I make mistakes—whether they're super small or SUPER BIG. Today, I need Your forgiveness for. . .

I want to shine my light for You, God, so others can see it. And I would like to help build up courage in others too. People I am praying for today. . .

EVEN THOUGH I AM A COURAGEOUS GIRL, I SOMETIMES WORRY ABOUT THINGS. RIGHT NOW I AM WORRIED ABOUT. . .

....
....
....
....

AREAS OF MY LIFE WHERE I COULD USE SOME EXTRA COURAGE INCLUDE. . .

....
....
....
....
....
....
....

The life of a courageous girl is quite busy. Here's what's going on in my life that I need to share with You, God. . .

....
....
....
....
....
....
....
....

THANK YOU, GOD, FOR MAKING ME A COURAGEOUS GIRL!

Thank You, God, for hearing my prayers! AMEN.

Jesus said to His followers, "If anyone wants to be My follower, he must forget about himself. He must take up his cross and follow Me."

MATTHEW 16:24

DATE:

Dear God. . . **»»**

YOU GIVE ME COURAGE JUST WHEN I NEED IT THE MOST. AND I AM SO
THANKFUL! I AM ALSO THANKFUL FOR. . .

You forgive me when I make
mistakes—whether they're super
small or SUPER BIG. Today, I need
Your forgiveness for. . .

I want to shine my light for
You, God, so others can
see it. And I would like to
help build up courage in
others too. People I am
praying for today. . .

EVEN THOUGH I AM A COURAGEOUS GIRL, I SOMETIMES WORRY ABOUT THINGS. RIGHT NOW I AM WORRIED ABOUT. . .

....

....

....

....

AREAS OF MY LIFE WHERE I COULD USE SOME EXTRA COURAGE INCLUDE. . .

....

....

....

....

....

....

....

The life of a courageous girl is quite busy. Here's what's going on in my life that I need to share with You, God. . .

....

....

....

....

....

....

....

THANK YOU, GOD, FOR MAKING ME A COURAGEOUS GIRL!

Thank You, God,
for hearing my prayers!
AMEN.

God always does what is right. He will not forget the work you did to help the Christians and the work you are still doing to help them. This shows your love for Christ.

HEBREWS 6:10

Dear God. . .

YOU GIVE ME COURAGE JUST WHEN I NEED IT THE MOST. AND I AM SO THANKFUL! I AM ALSO THANKFUL FOR. . .

You forgive me when I make mistakes—whether they're super small or SUPER BIG. Today, I need Your forgiveness for. . .

I want to shine my light for You, God, so others can see it. And I would like to help build up courage in others too. People I am praying for today. . .

EVEN THOUGH I AM A COURAGEOUS GIRL, I SOMETIMES WORRY ABOUT THINGS. RIGHT NOW I AM WORRIED ABOUT. . .

....
....
....
....

AREAS OF MY LIFE WHERE I COULD USE SOME EXTRA COURAGE INCLUDE. . .

....
....
....
....
....
....
....

The life of a courageous girl is quite busy. Here's what's going on in my life that I need to share with You, God. . .

....
....
....
....
....
....
....

THANK YOU, GOD, FOR MAKING ME A COURAGEOUS GIRL!

Thank You, God, for hearing my prayers! AMEN.

And my God will give you everything you need because of His great riches in Christ Jesus.

PHILIPPIANS 4:19

DATE:

Dear God. . .

YOU GIVE ME COURAGE JUST WHEN I NEED IT THE MOST. AND I AM SO
THANKFUL! I AM ALSO THANKFUL FOR. . .

You forgive me when I make mistakes—whether they're super small or SUPER BIG. Today, I need Your forgiveness for. . .

I want to shine my light for You, God, so others can see it. And I would like to help build up courage in others too. People I am praying for today. . .

EVEN THOUGH I AM A COURAGEOUS GIRL, I SOMETIMES WORRY ABOUT THINGS. RIGHT NOW I AM WORRIED ABOUT. . .

AREAS OF MY LIFE WHERE I COULD USE SOME EXTRA COURAGE INCLUDE. . .

The life of a courageous girl is quite busy. Here's what's going on in my life that I need to share with You, God. . .

THANK YOU, GOD, FOR MAKING ME A COURAGEOUS GIRL!

Thank You, God, for hearing my prayers! AMEN.

"Men do not light a lamp and put it under a basket. They put it on a table so it gives light to all in the house. Let your light shine in front of men. Then they will see the good things you do and will honor your Father Who is in heaven."

MATTHEW 5:15–16

YOU GIVE ME COURAGE JUST WHEN I NEED IT THE MOST. AND I AM SO
THANKFUL! I AM ALSO THANKFUL FOR. . .

You forgive me when I make
mistakes—whether they're super
small or SUPER BIG. Today, I need
Your forgiveness for. . .

I want to shine my light for
You, God, so others can
see it. And I would like to
help build up courage in
others too. People I am
praying for today. . .

EVEN THOUGH I AM A COURAGEOUS GIRL, I SOMETIMES
WORRY ABOUT THINGS. RIGHT NOW I AM WORRIED ABOUT. . .

....
....
....

AREAS OF MY LIFE WHERE I COULD USE SOME
EXTRA COURAGE INCLUDE. . .

The life of a courageous girl
is quite busy. Here's what's
going on in my life that I need
to share with You, God. . .

THANK YOU, GOD, FOR MAKING ME A
COURAGEOUS GIRL!

Thank You, God,
for hearing my prayers!
AMEN.

" 'For I know the plans I have for you,' says the
Lord, 'plans for well-being and not for
trouble, to give you a future and a hope.' "

JEREMIAH 29:11

Dear God. . . ≫

YOU GIVE ME COURAGE JUST WHEN I NEED IT THE MOST. AND I AM SO THANKFUL! I AM ALSO THANKFUL FOR. . .

....
....
....
....

You forgive me when I make mistakes—whether they're super small or SUPER BIG. Today, I need Your forgiveness for. . .

....
....
....
....
....
....
....
....

I want to shine my light for You, God, so others can see it. And I would like to help build up courage in others too. People I am praying for today. . .

....
....
....
....
....
....
....
....
....
....

EVEN THOUGH I AM A COURAGEOUS GIRL, I SOMETIMES WORRY ABOUT THINGS. RIGHT NOW I AM WORRIED ABOUT. . .

AREAS OF MY LIFE WHERE I COULD USE SOME EXTRA COURAGE INCLUDE. . .

The life of a courageous girl is quite busy. Here's what's going on in my life that I need to share with You, God. . .

THANK YOU, GOD, FOR MAKING ME A COURAGEOUS GIRL!

Thank You, God, for hearing my prayers! AMEN.

"But to you who are willing to listen, I say, love your enemies! Do good to those who hate you."

LUKE 6:27 NLT

DATE:

Dear God. . . ≫

YOU GIVE ME COURAGE JUST WHEN I NEED IT THE MOST. AND I AM SO
THANKFUL! I AM ALSO THANKFUL FOR. . .

You forgive me when I make
mistakes—whether they're super
small or SUPER BIG. Today, I need
Your forgiveness for. . .

I want to shine my light for
You, God, so others can
see it. And I would like to
help build up courage in
others too. People I am
praying for today. . .

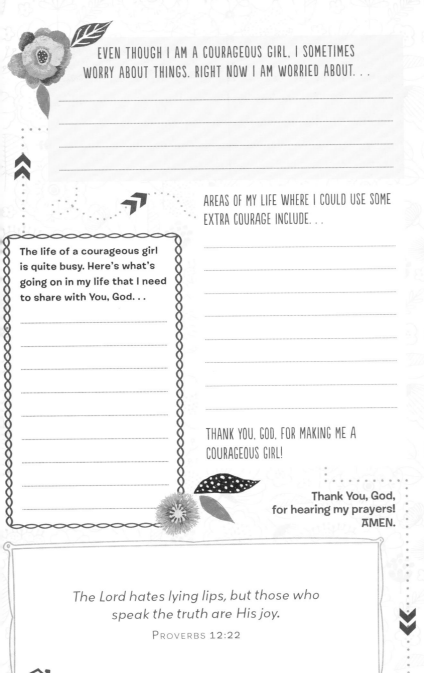

EVEN THOUGH I AM A COURAGEOUS GIRL, I SOMETIMES WORRY ABOUT THINGS. RIGHT NOW I AM WORRIED ABOUT. . .

AREAS OF MY LIFE WHERE I COULD USE SOME EXTRA COURAGE INCLUDE. . .

The life of a courageous girl is quite busy. Here's what's going on in my life that I need to share with You, God. . .

THANK YOU, GOD, FOR MAKING ME A COURAGEOUS GIRL!

Thank You, God, for hearing my prayers! AMEN.

The Lord hates lying lips, but those who speak the truth are His joy.

PROVERBS 12:22

Dear God. . .

YOU GIVE ME COURAGE JUST WHEN I NEED IT THE MOST. AND I AM SO THANKFUL! I AM ALSO THANKFUL FOR. . .

You forgive me when I make mistakes—whether they're super small or SUPER BIG. Today, I need Your forgiveness for. . .

I want to shine my light for You, God, so others can see it. And I would like to help build up courage in others too. People I am praying for today. . .

EVEN THOUGH I AM A COURAGEOUS GIRL, I SOMETIMES WORRY ABOUT THINGS. RIGHT NOW I AM WORRIED ABOUT. . .

....

....

....

....

AREAS OF MY LIFE WHERE I COULD USE SOME EXTRA COURAGE INCLUDE. . .

....

....

....

....

....

....

....

....

The life of a courageous girl is quite busy. Here's what's going on in my life that I need to share with You, God. . .

....

....

....

....

....

....

....

THANK YOU, GOD, FOR MAKING ME A COURAGEOUS GIRL!

Thank You, God, for hearing my prayers! AMEN.

"Do not let us be tempted, but keep us from sin."

MATTHEW 6:13

Dear God...

YOU GIVE ME COURAGE JUST WHEN I NEED IT THE MOST. AND I AM SO THANKFUL! I AM ALSO THANKFUL FOR. . .

....

....

....

....

....

You forgive me when I make mistakes—whether they're super small or SUPER BIG. Today, I need Your forgiveness for. . .

....

....

....

....

....

....

....

....

....

I want to shine my light for You, God, so others can see it. And I would like to help build up courage in others too. People I am praying for today. . .

....

....

....

....

....

....

....

....

....

....

EVEN THOUGH I AM A COURAGEOUS GIRL, I SOMETIMES
WORRY ABOUT THINGS. RIGHT NOW I AM WORRIED ABOUT. . .

....

....

....

....

AREAS OF MY LIFE WHERE I COULD USE SOME
EXTRA COURAGE INCLUDE. . .

....

....

....

....

....

....

....

**The life of a courageous girl
is quite busy. Here's what's
going on in my life that I need
to share with You, God. . .**

....

....

....

....

....

....

....

....

THANK YOU, GOD, FOR MAKING ME A
COURAGEOUS GIRL!

**Thank You, God,
for hearing my prayers!
AMEN.**

*The Lord GOD has put his Spirit in me, because the
LORD has appointed me to tell the good news to
the poor. He has sent me to comfort those whose
hearts are broken, to tell the captives they are free,
and to tell the prisoners they are released.*

ISAIAH 61:1 NCV

Dear God. . . ⟫

YOU GIVE ME COURAGE JUST WHEN I NEED IT THE MOST. AND I AM SO THANKFUL! I AM ALSO THANKFUL FOR. . .

You forgive me when I make mistakes—whether they're super small or SUPER BIG. Today, I need Your forgiveness for. . .

I want to shine my light for You, God, so others can see it. And I would like to help build up courage in others too. People I am praying for today. . .

EVEN THOUGH I AM A COURAGEOUS GIRL, I SOMETIMES WORRY ABOUT THINGS. RIGHT NOW I AM WORRIED ABOUT. . .

AREAS OF MY LIFE WHERE I COULD USE SOME EXTRA COURAGE INCLUDE. . .

The life of a courageous girl is quite busy. Here's what's going on in my life that I need to share with You, God. . .

THANK YOU, GOD, FOR MAKING ME A COURAGEOUS GIRL!

Thank You, God, for hearing my prayers! AMEN.

Love each other with genuine affection, and take delight in honoring each other.

ROMANS 12:10 NLT

Dear God...

YOU GIVE ME COURAGE JUST WHEN I NEED IT THE MOST. AND I AM SO
THANKFUL! I AM ALSO THANKFUL FOR. . .

....

....

....

....

You forgive me when I make
mistakes—whether they're super
small or SUPER BIG. Today, I need
Your forgiveness for. . .

....

....

....

....

....

....

....

....

....

I want to shine my light for
You, God, so others can
see it. And I would like to
help build up courage in
others too. People I am
praying for today. . .

....

....

....

....

....

....

....

....

....

....

....

....

EVEN THOUGH I AM A COURAGEOUS GIRL, I SOMETIMES WORRY ABOUT THINGS. RIGHT NOW I AM WORRIED ABOUT. . .

AREAS OF MY LIFE WHERE I COULD USE SOME EXTRA COURAGE INCLUDE. . .

The life of a courageous girl is quite busy. Here's what's going on in my life that I need to share with You, God. . .

THANK YOU, GOD, FOR MAKING ME A COURAGEOUS GIRL!

Thank You, God, for hearing my prayers! AMEN.

"But with God everything is possible."

MATTHEW 19:26 NLT

Dear God. . . ≫

YOU GIVE ME COURAGE JUST WHEN I NEED IT THE MOST. AND I AM SO THANKFUL! I AM ALSO THANKFUL FOR. . . ..

....

....

....

....

You forgive me when I make mistakes—whether they're super small or SUPER BIG. Today, I need Your forgiveness for. . .

....

....

....

....

....

....

....

....

....

....

I want to shine my light for You, God, so others can see it. And I would like to help build up courage in others too. People I am praying for today. . .

....

....

....

....

....

....

....

....

....

....

....

....

EVEN THOUGH I AM A COURAGEOUS GIRL, I SOMETIMES
WORRY ABOUT THINGS. RIGHT NOW I AM WORRIED ABOUT. . .

....

....

....

....

AREAS OF MY LIFE WHERE I COULD USE SOME
EXTRA COURAGE INCLUDE. . .

....

....

....

....

....

....

....

**The life of a courageous girl
is quite busy. Here's what's
going on in my life that I need
to share with You, God. . .**

....

....

....

....

....

....

....

THANK YOU, GOD, FOR MAKING ME A
COURAGEOUS GIRL!

**Thank You, God,
for hearing my prayers!
AMEN.**

*"If anyone wants to keep his life safe, he will lose it.
If anyone gives up his life because
of Me, he will save it."*

MATTHEW 16:25

Dear God. . . ➤➤

YOU GIVE ME COURAGE JUST WHEN I NEED IT THE MOST. AND I AM SO
THANKFUL! I AM ALSO THANKFUL FOR. . .

You forgive me when I make
mistakes—whether they're super
small or SUPER BIG. Today, I need
Your forgiveness for. . .

I want to shine my light for
You, God, so others can
see it. And I would like to
help build up courage in
others too. People I am
praying for today. . .

EVEN THOUGH I AM A COURAGEOUS GIRL, I SOMETIMES WORRY ABOUT THINGS. RIGHT NOW I AM WORRIED ABOUT. . .

AREAS OF MY LIFE WHERE I COULD USE SOME EXTRA COURAGE INCLUDE. . .

The life of a courageous girl is quite busy. Here's what's going on in my life that I need to share with You, God. . .

THANK YOU, GOD, FOR MAKING ME A COURAGEOUS GIRL!

Thank You, God, for hearing my prayers! AMEN.

"Be strong and have strength of heart! Do not be afraid or lose faith. For the Lord your God is with you anywhere you go."

JOSHUA 1:9

YOU GIVE ME COURAGE JUST WHEN I NEED IT THE MOST. AND I AM SO
THANKFUL! I AM ALSO THANKFUL FOR. . .

You forgive me when I make
mistakes—whether they're super
small or SUPER BIG. Today, I need
Your forgiveness for. . .

I want to shine my light for
You, God, so others can
see it. And I would like to
help build up courage in
others too. People I am
praying for today. . .

EVEN THOUGH I AM A COURAGEOUS GIRL, I SOMETIMES WORRY ABOUT THINGS. RIGHT NOW I AM WORRIED ABOUT. . .

AREAS OF MY LIFE WHERE I COULD USE SOME EXTRA COURAGE INCLUDE. . .

The life of a courageous girl is quite busy. Here's what's going on in my life that I need to share with You, God. . .

THANK YOU, GOD, FOR MAKING ME A COURAGEOUS GIRL!

Thank You, God, for hearing my prayers! AMEN.

LORD, even when I have trouble all around me, you will keep me alive. When my enemies are angry, you will reach down and save me by your power.

PSALM 138:7 NCV

Dear God. . .

YOU GIVE ME COURAGE JUST WHEN I NEED IT THE MOST. AND I AM SO THANKFUL! I AM ALSO THANKFUL FOR. . .

You forgive me when I make mistakes—whether they're super small or SUPER BIG. Today, I need Your forgiveness for. . .

I want to shine my light for You, God, so others can see it. And I would like to help build up courage in others too. People I am praying for today. . .

EVEN THOUGH I AM A COURAGEOUS GIRL, I SOMETIMES
WORRY ABOUT THINGS. RIGHT NOW I AM WORRIED ABOUT. . .

AREAS OF MY LIFE WHERE I COULD USE SOME
EXTRA COURAGE INCLUDE. . .

The life of a courageous girl
is quite busy. Here's what's
going on in my life that I need
to share with You, God. . .

THANK YOU, GOD, FOR MAKING ME A
COURAGEOUS GIRL!

Thank You, God,
for hearing my prayers!
AMEN.

*"Call to Me, and I will answer you. And I will show you
great and wonderful things which you do not know."*

JEREMIAH 33:3

Dear God. . . 〉〉

YOU GIVE ME COURAGE JUST WHEN I NEED IT THE MOST. AND I AM SO
THANKFUL! I AM ALSO THANKFUL FOR. . .

You forgive me when I make
mistakes—whether they're super
small or SUPER BIG. Today, I need
Your forgiveness for. . .

I want to shine my light for
You, God, so others can
see it. And I would like to
help build up courage in
others too. People I am
praying for today. . .

EVEN THOUGH I AM A COURAGEOUS GIRL, I SOMETIMES WORRY ABOUT THINGS. RIGHT NOW I AM WORRIED ABOUT. . .

AREAS OF MY LIFE WHERE I COULD USE SOME EXTRA COURAGE INCLUDE. . .

The life of a courageous girl is quite busy. Here's what's going on in my life that I need to share with You, God. . .

THANK YOU, GOD, FOR MAKING ME A COURAGEOUS GIRL!

Thank You, God, for hearing my prayers! AMEN.

Open your mouth for those who cannot speak, and for the rights of those who are left without help.

PROVERBS 31:8

DATE:

Dear God. . .

YOU GIVE ME COURAGE JUST WHEN I NEED IT THE MOST. AND I AM SO
THANKFUL! I AM ALSO THANKFUL FOR. . .

....

....

....

You forgive me when I make
mistakes—whether they're super
small or SUPER BIG. Today, I need
Your forgiveness for. . .

I want to shine my light for
You, God, so others can
see it. And I would like to
help build up courage in
others too. People I am
praying for today. . .

EVEN THOUGH I AM A COURAGEOUS GIRL, I SOMETIMES
WORRY ABOUT THINGS. RIGHT NOW I AM WORRIED ABOUT. . .

....

....

....

....

AREAS OF MY LIFE WHERE I COULD USE SOME
EXTRA COURAGE INCLUDE. . .

The life of a courageous girl
is quite busy. Here's what's
going on in my life that I need
to share with You, God. . .

THANK YOU, GOD, FOR MAKING ME A
COURAGEOUS GIRL!

Thank You, God,
for hearing my prayers!
AMEN.

*Be happy in your hope. Do not give up when trouble
comes. Do not let anything stop you from praying.*

ROMANS 12:12

Dear God. . . ›››

YOU GIVE ME COURAGE JUST WHEN I NEED IT THE MOST. AND I AM SO THANKFUL! I AM ALSO THANKFUL FOR. . .

....

....

....

....

You forgive me when I make mistakes—whether they're super small or SUPER BIG. Today, I need Your forgiveness for. . .

I want to shine my light for You, God, so others can see it. And I would like to help build up courage in others too. People I am praying for today. . .

EVEN THOUGH I AM A COURAGEOUS GIRL, I SOMETIMES
WORRY ABOUT THINGS. RIGHT NOW I AM WORRIED ABOUT. . .

....
....
....
....

AREAS OF MY LIFE WHERE I COULD USE SOME
EXTRA COURAGE INCLUDE. . .

....
....
....
....
....
....
....

The life of a courageous girl
is quite busy. Here's what's
going on in my life that I need
to share with You, God. . .

....
....
....
....
....
....
....

THANK YOU, GOD, FOR MAKING ME A
COURAGEOUS GIRL!

Thank You, God,
for hearing my prayers!
AMEN.

"For My thoughts are not your thoughts,
and My ways are not your ways," says the Lord.

ISAIAH 55:8

Dear God. . . »»

YOU GIVE ME COURAGE JUST WHEN I NEED IT THE MOST. AND I AM SO THANKFUL! I AM ALSO THANKFUL FOR. . .

You forgive me when I make mistakes—whether they're super small or SUPER BIG. Today, I need Your forgiveness for. . .

I want to shine my light for You, God, so others can see it. And I would like to help build up courage in others too. People I am praying for today. . .

EVEN THOUGH I AM A COURAGEOUS GIRL, I SOMETIMES
WORRY ABOUT THINGS. RIGHT NOW I AM WORRIED ABOUT. . .

AREAS OF MY LIFE WHERE I COULD USE SOME
EXTRA COURAGE INCLUDE. . .

The life of a courageous girl
is quite busy. Here's what's
going on in my life that I need
to share with You, God. . .

THANK YOU, GOD, FOR MAKING ME A
COURAGEOUS GIRL!

Thank You, God,
for hearing my prayers!
AMEN.

[Jesus] said. . . , "You are to go to all the world and
preach the Good News to every person."

MARK 16:15

DATE:

Dear God. . .

YOU GIVE ME COURAGE JUST WHEN I NEED IT THE MOST. AND I AM SO THANKFUL! I AM ALSO THANKFUL FOR. . .

You forgive me when I make mistakes—whether they're super small or SUPER BIG. Today, I need Your forgiveness for. . .

I want to shine my light for You, God, so others can see it. And I would like to help build up courage in others too. People I am praying for today. . .

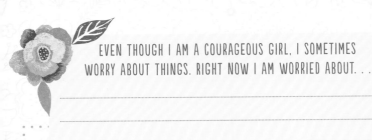

EVEN THOUGH I AM A COURAGEOUS GIRL, I SOMETIMES WORRY ABOUT THINGS. RIGHT NOW I AM WORRIED ABOUT. . .

....

....

....

....

AREAS OF MY LIFE WHERE I COULD USE SOME EXTRA COURAGE INCLUDE. . .

....

....

....

....

....

....

....

....

The life of a courageous girl is quite busy. Here's what's going on in my life that I need to share with You, God. . .

....

....

....

....

....

....

....

THANK YOU, GOD, FOR MAKING ME A COURAGEOUS GIRL!

Thank You, God, for hearing my prayers! AMEN.

God does not show favoritism.

ROMANS 2:11 NLT

Dear God. . . »

YOU GIVE ME COURAGE JUST WHEN I NEED IT THE MOST. AND I AM SO
THANKFUL! I AM ALSO THANKFUL FOR. . .

You forgive me when I make
mistakes—whether they're super
small or SUPER BIG. Today, I need
Your forgiveness for. . .

I want to shine my light for
You, God, so others can
see it. And I would like to
help build up courage in
others too. People I am
praying for today. . .

EVEN THOUGH I AM A COURAGEOUS GIRL, I SOMETIMES WORRY ABOUT THINGS. RIGHT NOW I AM WORRIED ABOUT. . .

....

....

....

AREAS OF MY LIFE WHERE I COULD USE SOME EXTRA COURAGE INCLUDE. . .

....

....

....

....

....

....

....

The life of a courageous girl is quite busy. Here's what's going on in my life that I need to share with You, God. . .

....

....

....

....

....

....

....

THANK YOU, GOD, FOR MAKING ME A COURAGEOUS GIRL!

Thank You, God, for hearing my prayers! AMEN.

"Whoever does not give up all that he has, cannot be My follower."

LUKE 14:33

YOU GIVE ME COURAGE JUST WHEN I NEED IT THE MOST. AND I AM SO THANKFUL! I AM ALSO THANKFUL FOR. . .

You forgive me when I make mistakes—whether they're super small or SUPER BIG. Today, I need Your forgiveness for. . .

I want to shine my light for You, God, so others can see it. And I would like to help build up courage in others too. People I am praying for today. . .

EVEN THOUGH I AM A COURAGEOUS GIRL, I SOMETIMES
WORRY ABOUT THINGS. RIGHT NOW I AM WORRIED ABOUT. . .

....

....

....

....

AREAS OF MY LIFE WHERE I COULD USE SOME
EXTRA COURAGE INCLUDE. . .

....

....

....

....

....

....

....

The life of a courageous girl
is quite busy. Here's what's
going on in my life that I need
to share with You, God. . .

....

....

....

....

....

....

THANK YOU, GOD, FOR MAKING ME A
COURAGEOUS GIRL!

Thank You, God,
for hearing my prayers!
AMEN.

"Ask, and what you are asking for will be given to you.
Look, and what you are looking for you will find.
Knock, and the door you are knocking
on will be opened to you."

MATTHEW 7:7

DATE:

Dear God. . .

YOU GIVE ME COURAGE JUST WHEN I NEED IT THE MOST. AND I AM SO THANKFUL! I AM ALSO THANKFUL FOR. . .

You forgive me when I make mistakes—whether they're super small or SUPER BIG. Today, I need Your forgiveness for. . .

I want to shine my light for You, God, so others can see it. And I would like to help build up courage in others too. People I am praying for today. . .

EVEN THOUGH I AM A COURAGEOUS GIRL, I SOMETIMES
WORRY ABOUT THINGS. RIGHT NOW I AM WORRIED ABOUT. . .

....

....

....

....

AREAS OF MY LIFE WHERE I COULD USE SOME
EXTRA COURAGE INCLUDE. . .

The life of a courageous girl
is quite busy. Here's what's
going on in my life that I need
to share with You, God. . .

....

....

....

....

....

....

....

....

THANK YOU, GOD, FOR MAKING ME A
COURAGEOUS GIRL!

Thank You, God,
for hearing my prayers!
AMEN.

*And so let us come near to God
with a true heart full of faith.*

HEBREWS 10:22

Dear God. . . ≫

YOU GIVE ME COURAGE JUST WHEN I NEED IT THE MOST. AND I AM SO
THANKFUL! I AM ALSO THANKFUL FOR. . .

You forgive me when I make
mistakes—whether they're super
small or SUPER BIG. Today, I need
Your forgiveness for. . .

I want to shine my light for
You, God, so others can
see it. And I would like to
help build up courage in
others too. People I am
praying for today. . .

EVEN THOUGH I AM A COURAGEOUS GIRL, I SOMETIMES
WORRY ABOUT THINGS. RIGHT NOW I AM WORRIED ABOUT. . .

....

....

....

....

AREAS OF MY LIFE WHERE I COULD USE SOME
EXTRA COURAGE INCLUDE. . .

....

....

....

....

....

....

....

The life of a courageous girl
is quite busy. Here's what's
going on in my life that I need
to share with You, God. . .

....

....

....

....

....

....

....

THANK YOU, GOD, FOR MAKING ME A
COURAGEOUS GIRL!

Thank You, God,
for hearing my prayers!
AMEN.

*All the days planned for me were written in
your book before I was one day old.*

PSALM 139:16 NCV

YOU GIVE ME COURAGE JUST WHEN I NEED IT THE MOST. AND I AM SO
THANKFUL! I AM ALSO THANKFUL FOR. . .

You forgive me when I make
mistakes—whether they're super
small or SUPER BIG. Today, I need
Your forgiveness for. . .

I want to shine my light for
You, God, so others can
see it. And I would like to
help build up courage in
others too. People I am
praying for today. . .

EVEN THOUGH I AM A COURAGEOUS GIRL, I SOMETIMES WORRY ABOUT THINGS. RIGHT NOW I AM WORRIED ABOUT. . .

....

....

....

....

AREAS OF MY LIFE WHERE I COULD USE SOME EXTRA COURAGE INCLUDE. . .

....

....

....

....

....

....

....

The life of a courageous girl is quite busy. Here's what's going on in my life that I need to share with You, God. . .

....

....

....

....

....

....

....

THANK YOU, GOD, FOR MAKING ME A COURAGEOUS GIRL!

Thank You, God, for hearing my prayers! AMEN.

"Don't worry and say, 'What will we eat?' or 'What will we drink?' or 'What will we wear?' . . . Seek first God's kingdom and what God wants. Then all your other needs will be met as well."

MATTHEW 6:31, 33 NCV

Dear God. . .

YOU GIVE ME COURAGE JUST WHEN I NEED IT THE MOST. AND I AM SO THANKFUL! I AM ALSO THANKFUL FOR. . .

You forgive me when I make mistakes—whether they're super small or SUPER BIG. Today, I need Your forgiveness for. . .

I want to shine my light for You, God, so others can see it. And I would like to help build up courage in others too. People I am praying for today. . .

EVEN THOUGH I AM A COURAGEOUS GIRL, I SOMETIMES
WORRY ABOUT THINGS. RIGHT NOW I AM WORRIED ABOUT. . .

....

....

....

AREAS OF MY LIFE WHERE I COULD USE SOME
EXTRA COURAGE INCLUDE. . .

....

....

....

....

....

....

The life of a courageous girl
is quite busy. Here's what's
going on in my life that I need
to share with You, God. . .

....

....

....

....

....

....

....

....

THANK YOU, GOD, FOR MAKING ME A
COURAGEOUS GIRL!

Thank You, God,
for hearing my prayers!
AMEN.

*The Lord is my light and the One Who saves me.
Whom should I fear? The Lord is the strength
of my life. Of whom should I be afraid?*

PSALM 27:1

Dear God... ≫

YOU GIVE ME COURAGE JUST WHEN I NEED IT THE MOST. AND I AM SO
THANKFUL! I AM ALSO THANKFUL FOR. . ...

....

....

....

....

You forgive me when I make
mistakes—whether they're super
small or SUPER BIG. Today, I need
Your forgiveness for. . .

....

....

....

....

....

....

....

....

....

....

....

I want to shine my light for
You, God, so others can
see it. And I would like to
help build up courage in
others too. People I am
praying for today. . .

....

....

....

....

....

....

....

....

....

....

....

EVEN THOUGH I AM A COURAGEOUS GIRL, I SOMETIMES WORRY ABOUT THINGS. RIGHT NOW I AM WORRIED ABOUT. . .

....

....

....

AREAS OF MY LIFE WHERE I COULD USE SOME EXTRA COURAGE INCLUDE. . .

....

....

....

....

....

....

....

The life of a courageous girl is quite busy. Here's what's going on in my life that I need to share with You, God. . .

....

....

....

....

....

....

....

THANK YOU, GOD, FOR MAKING ME A COURAGEOUS GIRL!

Thank You, God, for hearing my prayers! AMEN.

Follow my example, as I follow the example of Christ.

1 CORINTHIANS 11:1 NCV

YOU GIVE ME COURAGE JUST WHEN I NEED IT THE MOST. AND I AM SO THANKFUL! I AM ALSO THANKFUL FOR. . . ..

....

....

....

....

You forgive me when I make mistakes—whether they're super small or SUPER BIG. Today, I need Your forgiveness for. . .

....

....

....

....

....

....

....

....

....

....

I want to shine my light for You, God, so others can see it. And I would like to help build up courage in others too. People I am praying for today. . .

....

....

....

....

....

....

....

....

....

....

EVEN THOUGH I AM A COURAGEOUS GIRL, I SOMETIMES
WORRY ABOUT THINGS. RIGHT NOW I AM WORRIED ABOUT. . .

....

....

....

....

AREAS OF MY LIFE WHERE I COULD USE SOME
EXTRA COURAGE INCLUDE. . .

....

....

The life of a courageous girl
is quite busy. Here's what's
going on in my life that I need
to share with You, God. . .

....

....

....

....

....

....

THANK YOU, GOD, FOR MAKING ME A
COURAGEOUS GIRL!

Thank You, God,
for hearing my prayers!
AMEN.

*Be strong in the Lord and
in his mighty power.*

EPHESIANS 6:10 NLT

DATE:

Dear God. . .

YOU GIVE ME COURAGE JUST WHEN I NEED IT THE MOST. AND I AM SO THANKFUL! I AM ALSO THANKFUL FOR. . .

You forgive me when I make mistakes—whether they're super small or SUPER BIG. Today, I need Your forgiveness for. . .

I want to shine my light for You, God, so others can see it. And I would like to help build up courage in others too. People I am praying for today. . .

EVEN THOUGH I AM A COURAGEOUS GIRL, I SOMETIMES
WORRY ABOUT THINGS. RIGHT NOW I AM WORRIED ABOUT. . .

....

....

....

....

AREAS OF MY LIFE WHERE I COULD USE SOME
EXTRA COURAGE INCLUDE. . .

....

....

....

....

....

....

The life of a courageous girl
is quite busy. Here's what's
going on in my life that I need
to share with You, God. . .

....

....

....

....

....

....

THANK YOU, GOD, FOR MAKING ME A
COURAGEOUS GIRL!

Thank You, God,
for hearing my prayers!
AMEN.

*We know that God makes all things work together
for the good of those who love Him and
are chosen to be a part of His plan.*

ROMANS 8:28

DATE:

Dear God. . .

YOU GIVE ME COURAGE JUST WHEN I NEED IT THE MOST. AND I AM SO THANKFUL! I AM ALSO THANKFUL FOR. . .

You forgive me when I make mistakes—whether they're super small or SUPER BIG. Today, I need Your forgiveness for. . .

I want to shine my light for You, God, so others can see it. And I would like to help build up courage in others too. People I am praying for today. . .

EVEN THOUGH I AM A COURAGEOUS GIRL, I SOMETIMES WORRY ABOUT THINGS. RIGHT NOW I AM WORRIED ABOUT. . .

....

....

....

....

AREAS OF MY LIFE WHERE I COULD USE SOME EXTRA COURAGE INCLUDE. . .

The life of a courageous girl is quite busy. Here's what's going on in my life that I need to share with You, God. . .

....

....

....

....

....

....

....

....

THANK YOU, GOD, FOR MAKING ME A COURAGEOUS GIRL!

Thank You, God, for hearing my prayers! AMEN.

All things should be done in the right way, one after the other.

1 CORINTHIANS 14:40

Dear God...

YOU GIVE ME COURAGE JUST WHEN I NEED IT THE MOST. AND I AM SO THANKFUL! I AM ALSO THANKFUL FOR. . .

You forgive me when I make mistakes—whether they're super small or SUPER BIG. Today, I need Your forgiveness for. . .

I want to shine my light for You, God, so others can see it. And I would like to help build up courage in others too. People I am praying for today. . .

EVEN THOUGH I AM A COURAGEOUS GIRL, I SOMETIMES
WORRY ABOUT THINGS. RIGHT NOW I AM WORRIED ABOUT. . .

....

....

....

....

AREAS OF MY LIFE WHERE I COULD USE SOME
EXTRA COURAGE INCLUDE. . .

**The life of a courageous girl
is quite busy. Here's what's
going on in my life that I need
to share with You, God. . .**

....

....

....

....

....

....

....

....

....

THANK YOU, GOD, FOR MAKING ME A
COURAGEOUS GIRL!

**Thank You, God,
for hearing my prayers!
AMEN.**

Since God is for us, who can be against us?

ROMANS 8:31

Dear God. . . ≫

YOU GIVE ME COURAGE JUST WHEN I NEED IT THE MOST. AND I AM SO THANKFUL! I AM ALSO THANKFUL FOR. . .

You forgive me when I make mistakes—whether they're super small or SUPER BIG. Today, I need Your forgiveness for. . .

I want to shine my light for You, God, so others can see it. And I would like to help build up courage in others too. People I am praying for today. . .

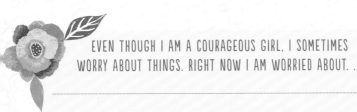

EVEN THOUGH I AM A COURAGEOUS GIRL, I SOMETIMES WORRY ABOUT THINGS. RIGHT NOW I AM WORRIED ABOUT. . .

AREAS OF MY LIFE WHERE I COULD USE SOME EXTRA COURAGE INCLUDE. . .

The life of a courageous girl is quite busy. Here's what's going on in my life that I need to share with You, God. . .

THANK YOU, GOD, FOR MAKING ME A COURAGEOUS GIRL!

Thank You, God, for hearing my prayers! AMEN.

"Bless those who curse you, pray for those who are cruel to you."

LUKE 6:28 NCV

YOU GIVE ME COURAGE JUST WHEN I NEED IT THE MOST. AND I AM SO THANKFUL! I AM ALSO THANKFUL FOR. . .

You forgive me when I make mistakes—whether they're super small or SUPER BIG. Today, I need Your forgiveness for. . .

I want to shine my light for You, God, so others can see it. And I would like to help build up courage in others too. People I am praying for today. . .

EVEN THOUGH I AM A COURAGEOUS GIRL, I SOMETIMES WORRY ABOUT THINGS. RIGHT NOW I AM WORRIED ABOUT...

....

....

....

....

AREAS OF MY LIFE WHERE I COULD USE SOME EXTRA COURAGE INCLUDE...

....

....

....

....

....

....

The life of a courageous girl is quite busy. Here's what's going on in my life that I need to share with You, God...

....

....

....

....

....

....

....

....

THANK YOU, GOD, FOR MAKING ME A COURAGEOUS GIRL!

Thank You, God, for hearing my prayers! AMEN.

He gives strength to the weak. And He gives power to him who has little strength.

ISAIAH 40:29

DATE:

Dear God. . .

YOU GIVE ME COURAGE JUST WHEN I NEED IT THE MOST. AND I AM SO THANKFUL! I AM ALSO THANKFUL FOR. . .

You forgive me when I make mistakes—whether they're super small or SUPER BIG. Today, I need Your forgiveness for. . .

I want to shine my light for You, God, so others can see it. And I would like to help build up courage in others too. People I am praying for today. . .

EVEN THOUGH I AM A COURAGEOUS GIRL, I SOMETIMES
WORRY ABOUT THINGS. RIGHT NOW I AM WORRIED ABOUT. . .

....

....

....

....

AREAS OF MY LIFE WHERE I COULD USE SOME
EXTRA COURAGE INCLUDE. . .

The life of a courageous girl
is quite busy. Here's what's
going on in my life that I need
to share with You, God. . .

....

....

....

....

....

....

....

THANK YOU, GOD, FOR MAKING ME A
COURAGEOUS GIRL!

Thank You, God,
for hearing my prayers!
AMEN.

Some friends may ruin you, but a real friend
will be more loyal than a brother.

PROVERBS 18:24 NCV

DATE:

Dear God... »

YOU GIVE ME COURAGE JUST WHEN I NEED IT THE MOST. AND I AM SO
THANKFUL! I AM ALSO THANKFUL FOR. . .

You forgive me when I make
mistakes—whether they're super
small or SUPER BIG. Today, I need
Your forgiveness for. . .

I want to shine my light for
You, God, so others can
see it. And I would like to
help build up courage in
others too. People I am
praying for today. . .

EVEN THOUGH I AM A COURAGEOUS GIRL, I SOMETIMES
WORRY ABOUT THINGS. RIGHT NOW I AM WORRIED ABOUT. . .

....

....

....

....

AREAS OF MY LIFE WHERE I COULD USE SOME
EXTRA COURAGE INCLUDE. . .

....

....

....

....

....

....

....

The life of a courageous girl
is quite busy. Here's what's
going on in my life that I need
to share with You, God. . .

....

....

....

....

....

....

....

THANK YOU, GOD, FOR MAKING ME A
COURAGEOUS GIRL!

**Thank You, God,
for hearing my prayers!
AMEN.**

*The Lord God helps me, so I will not be ashamed.
I will be determined, and I know
I will not be disgraced.*

ISAIAH 50:7 NCV

DATE:

Dear God...

YOU GIVE ME COURAGE JUST WHEN I NEED IT THE MOST. AND I AM SO THANKFUL! I AM ALSO THANKFUL FOR. . .

You forgive me when I make mistakes—whether they're super small or SUPER BIG. Today, I need Your forgiveness for. . .

I want to shine my light for You, God, so others can see it. And I would like to help build up courage in others too. People I am praying for today. . .

EVEN THOUGH I AM A COURAGEOUS GIRL, I SOMETIMES
WORRY ABOUT THINGS. RIGHT NOW I AM WORRIED ABOUT. . .

....

....

....

....

AREAS OF MY LIFE WHERE I COULD USE SOME
EXTRA COURAGE INCLUDE. . .

The life of a courageous girl
is quite busy. Here's what's
going on in my life that I need
to share with You, God. . .

THANK YOU, GOD, FOR MAKING ME A
COURAGEOUS GIRL!

Thank You, God,
for hearing my prayers!
AMEN.

It is better not to make a promise,
than to make a promise and not pay it.

ECCLESIASTES 5:5

Dear God. . .

YOU GIVE ME COURAGE JUST WHEN I NEED IT THE MOST. AND I AM SO
THANKFUL! I AM ALSO THANKFUL FOR. . .

You forgive me when I make
mistakes—whether they're super
small or SUPER BIG. Today, I need
Your forgiveness for. . .

I want to shine my light for
You, God, so others can
see it. And I would like to
help build up courage in
others too. People I am
praying for today. . .

EVEN THOUGH I AM A COURAGEOUS GIRL, I SOMETIMES
WORRY ABOUT THINGS. RIGHT NOW I AM WORRIED ABOUT. . .

AREAS OF MY LIFE WHERE I COULD USE SOME
EXTRA COURAGE INCLUDE. . .

The life of a courageous girl
is quite busy. Here's what's
going on in my life that I need
to share with You, God. . .

THANK YOU, GOD, FOR MAKING ME A
COURAGEOUS GIRL!

Thank You, God,
for hearing my prayers!
AMEN.

LORD, you have examined me
and know all about me.

PSALM 139:1 NCV

Dear God. . . »

YOU GIVE ME COURAGE JUST WHEN I NEED IT THE MOST. AND I AM SO THANKFUL! I AM ALSO THANKFUL FOR. . .

You forgive me when I make mistakes—whether they're super small or SUPER BIG. Today, I need Your forgiveness for. . .

I want to shine my light for You, God, so others can see it. And I would like to help build up courage in others too. People I am praying for today. . .

EVEN THOUGH I AM A COURAGEOUS GIRL, I SOMETIMES WORRY ABOUT THINGS. RIGHT NOW I AM WORRIED ABOUT. . .

AREAS OF MY LIFE WHERE I COULD USE SOME EXTRA COURAGE INCLUDE. . .

The life of a courageous girl is quite busy. Here's what's going on in my life that I need to share with You, God. . .

THANK YOU, GOD, FOR MAKING ME A COURAGEOUS GIRL!

Thank You, God, for hearing my prayers! AMEN.

But it is no shame to suffer for being a Christian. Praise God for the privilege of being called by his name!

1 PETER 4:16 NLT

Dear God. . . »

YOU GIVE ME COURAGE JUST WHEN I NEED IT THE MOST. AND I AM SO
THANKFUL! I AM ALSO THANKFUL FOR. . .

....

....

....

....

You forgive me when I make
mistakes—whether they're super
small or SUPER BIG. Today, I need
Your forgiveness for. . .

....

....

....

....

....

....

....

....

....

I want to shine my light for
You, God, so others can
see it. And I would like to
help build up courage in
others too. People I am
praying for today. . .

....

....

....

....

....

....

....

....

....

....

EVEN THOUGH I AM A COURAGEOUS GIRL, I SOMETIMES
WORRY ABOUT THINGS. RIGHT NOW I AM WORRIED ABOUT. . .

AREAS OF MY LIFE WHERE I COULD USE SOME
EXTRA COURAGE INCLUDE. . .

The life of a courageous girl
is quite busy. Here's what's
going on in my life that I need
to share with You, God. . .

THANK YOU, GOD, FOR MAKING ME A
COURAGEOUS GIRL!

Thank You, God,
for hearing my prayers!
AMEN.

*Respect your father and mother. This is the first Law
given that had a promise. The promise is this: If you
respect your father and mother, you will live a long
time and your life will be full of many good things.*

EPHESIANS 6:2–3

YOU GIVE ME COURAGE JUST WHEN I NEED IT THE MOST. AND I AM SO
THANKFUL! I AM ALSO THANKFUL FOR. . .

You forgive me when I make
mistakes—whether they're super
small or SUPER BIG. Today, I need
Your forgiveness for. . .

I want to shine my light for
You, God, so others can
see it. And I would like to
help build up courage in
others too. People I am
praying for today. . .

EVEN THOUGH I AM A COURAGEOUS GIRL, I SOMETIMES
WORRY ABOUT THINGS. RIGHT NOW I AM WORRIED ABOUT. . .

AREAS OF MY LIFE WHERE I COULD USE SOME
EXTRA COURAGE INCLUDE. . .

The life of a courageous girl
is quite busy. Here's what's
going on in my life that I need
to share with You, God. . .

THANK YOU, GOD, FOR MAKING ME A
COURAGEOUS GIRL!

Thank You, God,
for hearing my prayers!
AMEN.

"For God can do all things."

LUKE 1:37

YOU GIVE ME COURAGE JUST WHEN I NEED IT THE MOST. AND I AM SO
THANKFUL! I AM ALSO THANKFUL FOR. . .

You forgive me when I make
mistakes—whether they're super
small or SUPER BIG. Today, I need
Your forgiveness for. . .

I want to shine my light for
You, God, so others can
see it. And I would like to
help build up courage in
others too. People I am
praying for today. . .

EVEN THOUGH I AM A COURAGEOUS GIRL, I SOMETIMES WORRY ABOUT THINGS. RIGHT NOW I AM WORRIED ABOUT. . .

....

....

....

....

AREAS OF MY LIFE WHERE I COULD USE SOME EXTRA COURAGE INCLUDE. . .

....

....

....

....

....

....

....

The life of a courageous girl is quite busy. Here's what's going on in my life that I need to share with You, God. . .

....

....

....

....

....

....

....

....

THANK YOU, GOD, FOR MAKING ME A COURAGEOUS GIRL!

Thank You, God, for hearing my prayers! AMEN.

Do not forget to be kind to strangers and let them stay in your home. Some people have had angels in their homes without knowing it.

HEBREWS 13:2

Dear God...

YOU GIVE ME COURAGE JUST WHEN I NEED IT THE MOST. AND I AM SO THANKFUL! I AM ALSO THANKFUL FOR. . .

You forgive me when I make mistakes—whether they're super small or SUPER BIG. Today, I need Your forgiveness for. . .

I want to shine my light for You, God, so others can see it. And I would like to help build up courage in others too. People I am praying for today. . .

EVEN THOUGH I AM A COURAGEOUS GIRL, I SOMETIMES
WORRY ABOUT THINGS. RIGHT NOW I AM WORRIED ABOUT. . .

....

....

....

....

AREAS OF MY LIFE WHERE I COULD USE SOME
EXTRA COURAGE INCLUDE. . .

....

....

....

....

....

....

....

The life of a courageous girl
is quite busy. Here's what's
going on in my life that I need
to share with You, God. . .

....

....

....

....

....

....

....

THANK YOU, GOD, FOR MAKING ME A
COURAGEOUS GIRL!

Thank You, God,
for hearing my prayers!
AMEN.

"You will be a blessing to others."

GENESIS 12:2 NCV

DATE:

Dear God. . . . . . ➤➤

YOU GIVE ME COURAGE JUST WHEN I NEED IT THE MOST. AND I AM SO
THANKFUL! I AM ALSO THANKFUL FOR. . .

You forgive me when I make
mistakes—whether they're super
small or SUPER BIG. Today, I need
Your forgiveness for. . .

I want to shine my light for
You, God, so others can
see it. And I would like to
help build up courage in
others too. People I am
praying for today. . .

EVEN THOUGH I AM A COURAGEOUS GIRL, I SOMETIMES
WORRY ABOUT THINGS. RIGHT NOW I AM WORRIED ABOUT. . .

....

....

....

....

AREAS OF MY LIFE WHERE I COULD USE SOME
EXTRA COURAGE INCLUDE. . .

The life of a courageous girl
is quite busy. Here's what's
going on in my life that I need
to share with You, God. . .

....

....

....

....

....

....

....

THANK YOU, GOD, FOR MAKING ME A
COURAGEOUS GIRL!

Thank You, God,
for hearing my prayers!
AMEN.

*For You are good and ready to forgive, O Lord.
You are rich in loving-kindness to all who call to You.*

PSALM 86:5

DATE:

Dear God. . . »

YOU GIVE ME COURAGE JUST WHEN I NEED IT THE MOST. AND I AM SO
THANKFUL! I AM ALSO THANKFUL FOR. . .

You forgive me when I make
mistakes—whether they're super
small or SUPER BIG. Today, I need
Your forgiveness for. . .

I want to shine my light for
You, God, so others can
see it. And I would like to
help build up courage in
others too. People I am
praying for today. . .

EVEN THOUGH I AM A COURAGEOUS GIRL, I SOMETIMES WORRY ABOUT THINGS. RIGHT NOW I AM WORRIED ABOUT. . .

AREAS OF MY LIFE WHERE I COULD USE SOME EXTRA COURAGE INCLUDE. . .

The life of a courageous girl is quite busy. Here's what's going on in my life that I need to share with You, God. . .

THANK YOU, GOD, FOR MAKING ME A COURAGEOUS GIRL!

Thank You, God, for hearing my prayers! AMEN.

There is a special time for everything. There is a time for everything that happens under heaven.

ECCLESIASTES 3:1

Dear God. . . »»

YOU GIVE ME COURAGE JUST WHEN I NEED IT THE MOST. AND I AM SO THANKFUL! I AM ALSO THANKFUL FOR. . .

You forgive me when I make mistakes—whether they're super small or SUPER BIG. Today, I need Your forgiveness for. . .

I want to shine my light for You, God, so others can see it. And I would like to help build up courage in others too. People I am praying for today. . .

EVEN THOUGH I AM A COURAGEOUS GIRL, I SOMETIMES WORRY ABOUT THINGS. RIGHT NOW I AM WORRIED ABOUT. . .

....

....

....

....

AREAS OF MY LIFE WHERE I COULD USE SOME EXTRA COURAGE INCLUDE. . .

The life of a courageous girl is quite busy. Here's what's going on in my life that I need to share with You, God. . .

THANK YOU, GOD, FOR MAKING ME A COURAGEOUS GIRL!

Thank You, God, for hearing my prayers! AMEN.

Sing to the Lord a new song. Let all the earth sing to the Lord. Sing to the Lord. Honor His name. Make His saving power known from day to day.

PSALM 96:1-2

YOU GIVE ME COURAGE JUST WHEN I NEED IT THE MOST. AND I AM SO THANKFUL! I AM ALSO THANKFUL FOR. . .

You forgive me when I make mistakes—whether they're super small or SUPER BIG. Today, I need Your forgiveness for. . .

I want to shine my light for You, God, so others can see it. And I would like to help build up courage in others too. People I am praying for today. . .

EVEN THOUGH I AM A COURAGEOUS GIRL, I SOMETIMES
WORRY ABOUT THINGS. RIGHT NOW I AM WORRIED ABOUT. . .

....

....

....

AREAS OF MY LIFE WHERE I COULD USE SOME
EXTRA COURAGE INCLUDE. . .

....

....

....

....

The life of a courageous girl
is quite busy. Here's what's
going on in my life that I need
to share with You, God. . .

....

....

....

....

....

....

....

THANK YOU, GOD, FOR MAKING ME A
COURAGEOUS GIRL!

Thank You, God,
for hearing my prayers!
AMEN.

*I am happy to be weak and have troubles
so I can have Christ's power in me.*

2 CORINTHIANS 12:9

YOU GIVE ME COURAGE JUST WHEN I NEED IT THE MOST. AND I AM SO
THANKFUL! I AM ALSO THANKFUL FOR. . .

You forgive me when I make
mistakes—whether they're super
small or SUPER BIG. Today, I need
Your forgiveness for. . .

I want to shine my light for
You, God, so others can
see it. And I would like to
help build up courage in
others too. People I am
praying for today. . .

EVEN THOUGH I AM A COURAGEOUS GIRL, I SOMETIMES WORRY ABOUT THINGS. RIGHT NOW I AM WORRIED ABOUT. . .

....

....

....

....

AREAS OF MY LIFE WHERE I COULD USE SOME EXTRA COURAGE INCLUDE. . .

....

....

....

....

....

....

....

The life of a courageous girl is quite busy. Here's what's going on in my life that I need to share with You, God. . .

....

....

....

....

....

....

....

THANK YOU, GOD, FOR MAKING ME A COURAGEOUS GIRL!

Thank You, God, for hearing my prayers! AMEN.

How beautiful on the mountains are the feet of the messenger who brings good news, the good news of peace and salvation, the news that the God of Israel reigns!

ISAIAH 52:7 NLT

Dear God. . . »

YOU GIVE ME COURAGE JUST WHEN I NEED IT THE MOST. AND I AM SO
THANKFUL! I AM ALSO THANKFUL FOR. . .

You forgive me when I make
mistakes—whether they're super
small or SUPER BIG. Today, I need
Your forgiveness for. . .

I want to shine my light for
You, God, so others can
see it. And I would like to
help build up courage in
others too. People I am
praying for today. . .

EVEN THOUGH I AM A COURAGEOUS GIRL, I SOMETIMES WORRY ABOUT THINGS. RIGHT NOW I AM WORRIED ABOUT. . .

AREAS OF MY LIFE WHERE I COULD USE SOME EXTRA COURAGE INCLUDE. . .

The life of a courageous girl is quite busy. Here's what's going on in my life that I need to share with You, God. . .

THANK YOU, GOD, FOR MAKING ME A COURAGEOUS GIRL!

Thank You, God, for hearing my prayers! AMEN.

I will say to the Lord, "You are my safe and strong place, my God, in Whom I trust."

PSALM 91:2

Dear God. . .

YOU GIVE ME COURAGE JUST WHEN I NEED IT THE MOST. AND I AM SO THANKFUL! I AM ALSO THANKFUL FOR. . .

You forgive me when I make mistakes—whether they're super small or SUPER BIG. Today, I need Your forgiveness for. . .

I want to shine my light for You, God, so others can see it. And I would like to help build up courage in others too. People I am praying for today. . .

EVEN THOUGH I AM A COURAGEOUS GIRL, I SOMETIMES
WORRY ABOUT THINGS. RIGHT NOW I AM WORRIED ABOUT. . .

....

....

....

....

AREAS OF MY LIFE WHERE I COULD USE SOME
EXTRA COURAGE INCLUDE. . .

The life of a courageous girl
is quite busy. Here's what's
going on in my life that I need
to share with You, God. . .

....

....

....

....

....

....

....

....

....

THANK YOU, GOD, FOR MAKING ME A
COURAGEOUS GIRL!

Thank You, God,
for hearing my prayers!
AMEN.

Happy is the man who cares for the poor.
The Lord will save him in times of trouble.

PSALM 41:1

YOU GIVE ME COURAGE JUST WHEN I NEED IT THE MOST. AND I AM SO
THANKFUL! I AM ALSO THANKFUL FOR. . .

You forgive me when I make
mistakes—whether they're super
small or SUPER BIG. Today, I need
Your forgiveness for. . .

I want to shine my light for
You, God, so others can
see it. And I would like to
help build up courage in
others too. People I am
praying for today. . .

EVEN THOUGH I AM A COURAGEOUS GIRL, I SOMETIMES
WORRY ABOUT THINGS. RIGHT NOW I AM WORRIED ABOUT. . .

AREAS OF MY LIFE WHERE I COULD USE SOME
EXTRA COURAGE INCLUDE. . .

The life of a courageous girl
is quite busy. Here's what's
going on in my life that I need
to share with You, God. . .

THANK YOU, GOD, FOR MAKING ME A
COURAGEOUS GIRL!

Thank You, God,
for hearing my prayers!
AMEN.

*Choose my instruction rather than silver,
and knowledge rather than pure gold.*

PROVERBS 8:10 NLT

YOU GIVE ME COURAGE JUST WHEN I NEED IT THE MOST. AND I AM SO THANKFUL! I AM ALSO THANKFUL FOR. . .

You forgive me when I make mistakes—whether they're super small or SUPER BIG. Today, I need Your forgiveness for. . .

I want to shine my light for You, God, so others can see it. And I would like to help build up courage in others too. People I am praying for today. . .

EVEN THOUGH I AM A COURAGEOUS GIRL, I SOMETIMES WORRY ABOUT THINGS. RIGHT NOW I AM WORRIED ABOUT. . .

AREAS OF MY LIFE WHERE I COULD USE SOME EXTRA COURAGE INCLUDE. . .

The life of a courageous girl is quite busy. Here's what's going on in my life that I need to share with You, God. . .

THANK YOU, GOD, FOR MAKING ME A COURAGEOUS GIRL!

Thank You, God,
for hearing my prayers!
AMEN.

"You will know the truth and the truth will make you free."

JOHN 8:32

DATE: _____

Dear God...

YOU GIVE ME COURAGE JUST WHEN I NEED IT THE MOST. AND I AM SO
THANKFUL! I AM ALSO THANKFUL FOR. . .

_____
_____
_____
_____

You forgive me when I make
mistakes—whether they're super
small or SUPER BIG. Today, I need
Your forgiveness for. . .

_____
_____
_____
_____
_____
_____
_____
_____
_____

I want to shine my light for
You, God, so others can
see it. And I would like to
help build up courage in
others too. People I am
praying for today. . .

_____
_____
_____
_____
_____
_____
_____
_____
_____
_____
_____

EVEN THOUGH I AM A COURAGEOUS GIRL, I SOMETIMES WORRY ABOUT THINGS. RIGHT NOW I AM WORRIED ABOUT. . .

....

....

....

....

AREAS OF MY LIFE WHERE I COULD USE SOME EXTRA COURAGE INCLUDE. . .

The life of a courageous girl is quite busy. Here's what's going on in my life that I need to share with You, God. . .

....

....

....

....

....

....

....

....

....

....

....

....

....

....

....

....

THANK YOU, GOD, FOR MAKING ME A COURAGEOUS GIRL!

Thank You, God, for hearing my prayers! AMEN.

Live this free life by loving and helping others.

GALATIANS 5:13

DATE:

Dear God. . .

YOU GIVE ME COURAGE JUST WHEN I NEED IT THE MOST. AND I AM SO THANKFUL! I AM ALSO THANKFUL FOR. . .

You forgive me when I make mistakes—whether they're super small or SUPER BIG. Today, I need Your forgiveness for. . .

I want to shine my light for You, God, so others can see it. And I would like to help build up courage in others too. People I am praying for today. . .

EVEN THOUGH I AM A COURAGEOUS GIRL, I SOMETIMES
WORRY ABOUT THINGS. RIGHT NOW I AM WORRIED ABOUT. . .

....

....

....

....

AREAS OF MY LIFE WHERE I COULD USE SOME
EXTRA COURAGE INCLUDE. . .

The life of a courageous girl
is quite busy. Here's what's
going on in my life that I need
to share with You, God. . .

THANK YOU, GOD, FOR MAKING ME A
COURAGEOUS GIRL!

Thank You, God,
for hearing my prayers!
AMEN.

*"My life is worth nothing to me unless I use it for
finishing the work assigned me by the Lord Jesus—
the work of telling others the Good News
about the wonderful grace of God."*

ACTS 20:24 NLT

YOU GIVE ME COURAGE JUST WHEN I NEED IT THE MOST. AND I AM SO
THANKFUL! I AM ALSO THANKFUL FOR. . ...

....

....

....

....

You forgive me when I make
mistakes—whether they're super
small or SUPER BIG. Today, I need
Your forgiveness for. . .

....

....

....

....

....

....

....

....

....

....

I want to shine my light for
You, God, so others can
see it. And I would like to
help build up courage in
others too. People I am
praying for today. . .

....

....

....

....

....

....

....

....

....

....

....

....

EVEN THOUGH I AM A COURAGEOUS GIRL, I SOMETIMES
WORRY ABOUT THINGS. RIGHT NOW I AM WORRIED ABOUT. . .

....
....
....
....

AREAS OF MY LIFE WHERE I COULD USE SOME
EXTRA COURAGE INCLUDE. . .

The life of a courageous girl
is quite busy. Here's what's
going on in my life that I need
to share with You, God. . .

....
....
....
....
....
....
....

....
....
....
....
....

THANK YOU, GOD, FOR MAKING ME A
COURAGEOUS GIRL!

**Thank You, God,
for hearing my prayers!
AMEN.**

*So when the name of Jesus is spoken, everyone
in heaven and on earth and under the earth will
bow down before Him. And every tongue will
say Jesus Christ is Lord. Everyone will
give honor to God the Father.*

PHILIPPIANS 2:10–11

YOU GIVE ME COURAGE JUST WHEN I NEED IT THE MOST. AND I AM SO
THANKFUL! I AM ALSO THANKFUL FOR. . .

You forgive me when I make
mistakes—whether they're super
small or SUPER BIG. Today, I need
Your forgiveness for. . .

I want to shine my light for
You, God, so others can
see it. And I would like to
help build up courage in
others too. People I am
praying for today. . .

EVEN THOUGH I AM A COURAGEOUS GIRL, I SOMETIMES WORRY ABOUT THINGS. RIGHT NOW I AM WORRIED ABOUT...

....

....

....

AREAS OF MY LIFE WHERE I COULD USE SOME EXTRA COURAGE INCLUDE...

....

....

....

....

....

....

....

The life of a courageous girl is quite busy. Here's what's going on in my life that I need to share with You, God...

....

....

....

....

....

....

....

....

THANK YOU, GOD, FOR MAKING ME A COURAGEOUS GIRL!

Thank You, God, for hearing my prayers! AMEN.

"For God so loved the world that He gave His only Son. Whoever puts his trust in God's Son will not be lost but will have life that lasts forever."

JOHN 3:16

Dear God. . . ≫

YOU GIVE ME COURAGE JUST WHEN I NEED IT THE MOST. AND I AM SO
THANKFUL! I AM ALSO THANKFUL FOR. . .

You forgive me when I make
mistakes—whether they're super
small or SUPER BIG. Today, I need
Your forgiveness for. . .

I want to shine my light for
You, God, so others can
see it. And I would like to
help build up courage in
others too. People I am
praying for today. . .

EVEN THOUGH I AM A COURAGEOUS GIRL, I SOMETIMES
WORRY ABOUT THINGS. RIGHT NOW I AM WORRIED ABOUT. . .

....

....

....

....

AREAS OF MY LIFE WHERE I COULD USE SOME
EXTRA COURAGE INCLUDE. . .

....

....

....

....

....

....

....

**The life of a courageous girl
is quite busy. Here's what's
going on in my life that I need
to share with You, God. . .**

....

....

....

....

....

....

....

THANK YOU, GOD, FOR MAKING ME A
COURAGEOUS GIRL!

**Thank You, God,
for hearing my prayers!
AMEN.**

*If we tell Him our sins, He is faithful and we
can depend on Him to forgive us of our sins.
He will make our lives clean from all sin.*

1 JOHN 1:9

YOU GIVE ME COURAGE JUST WHEN I NEED IT THE MOST. AND I AM SO THANKFUL! I AM ALSO THANKFUL FOR. . . ..

....

....

....

....

You forgive me when I make mistakes—whether they're super small or SUPER BIG. Today, I need Your forgiveness for. . .

....

....

....

....

....

....

....

....

....

....

I want to shine my light for You, God, so others can see it. And I would like to help build up courage in others too. People I am praying for today. . .

....

....

....

....

....

....

....

....

....

....

....

....

EVEN THOUGH I AM A COURAGEOUS GIRL, I SOMETIMES
WORRY ABOUT THINGS. RIGHT NOW I AM WORRIED ABOUT. . .

....

....

....

....

AREAS OF MY LIFE WHERE I COULD USE SOME
EXTRA COURAGE INCLUDE. . .

The life of a courageous girl
is quite busy. Here's what's
going on in my life that I need
to share with You, God. . .

....

....

....

....

....

....

....

....

THANK YOU, GOD, FOR MAKING ME A
COURAGEOUS GIRL!

**Thank You, God,
for hearing my prayers!
AMEN.**

Keep a strong hold on your faith in Christ.

1 TIMOTHY 1:19

YOU GIVE ME COURAGE JUST WHEN I NEED IT THE MOST. AND I AM SO THANKFUL! I AM ALSO THANKFUL FOR. . .

You forgive me when I make mistakes—whether they're super small or SUPER BIG. Today, I need Your forgiveness for. . .

I want to shine my light for You, God, so others can see it. And I would like to help build up courage in others too. People I am praying for today. . .

EVEN THOUGH I AM A COURAGEOUS GIRL, I SOMETIMES
WORRY ABOUT THINGS. RIGHT NOW I AM WORRIED ABOUT. . .

....

....

....

....

AREAS OF MY LIFE WHERE I COULD USE SOME
EXTRA COURAGE INCLUDE. . .

The life of a courageous girl
is quite busy. Here's what's
going on in my life that I need
to share with You, God. . .

....

....

....

....

....

....

....

....

THANK YOU, GOD, FOR MAKING ME A
COURAGEOUS GIRL!

Thank You, God,
for hearing my prayers!
AMEN.

"Look for the Lord your God. And you will find Him
if you look for Him with all your heart and soul."

DEUTERONOMY 4:29

YOU GIVE ME COURAGE JUST WHEN I NEED IT THE MOST. AND I AM SO
THANKFUL! I AM ALSO THANKFUL FOR. . ...

....

....

....

....

You forgive me when I make
mistakes—whether they're super
small or SUPER BIG. Today, I need
Your forgiveness for. . .

....

....

....

....

....

....

....

....

....

I want to shine my light for
You, God, so others can
see it. And I would like to
help build up courage in
others too. People I am
praying for today. . .

....

....

....

....

....

....

....

....

....

....

....

EVEN THOUGH I AM A COURAGEOUS GIRL, I SOMETIMES
WORRY ABOUT THINGS. RIGHT NOW I AM WORRIED ABOUT. . .

....

....

....

....

AREAS OF MY LIFE WHERE I COULD USE SOME
EXTRA COURAGE INCLUDE. . .

**The life of a courageous girl
is quite busy. Here's what's
going on in my life that I need
to share with You, God. . .**

THANK YOU, GOD, FOR MAKING ME A
COURAGEOUS GIRL!

**Thank You, God,
for hearing my prayers!
AMEN.**

*[God] is like a rock; what he does is perfect,
and he is always fair.*

DEUTERONOMY 32:4 NCV

YOU GIVE ME COURAGE JUST WHEN I NEED IT THE MOST. AND I AM SO THANKFUL! I AM ALSO THANKFUL FOR. . .

You forgive me when I make mistakes—whether they're super small or SUPER BIG. Today, I need Your forgiveness for. . .

I want to shine my light for You, God, so others can see it. And I would like to help build up courage in others too. People I am praying for today. . .

EVEN THOUGH I AM A COURAGEOUS GIRL, I SOMETIMES
WORRY ABOUT THINGS. RIGHT NOW I AM WORRIED ABOUT. . .

....

....

....

....

AREAS OF MY LIFE WHERE I COULD USE SOME
EXTRA COURAGE INCLUDE. . .

**The life of a courageous girl
is quite busy. Here's what's
going on in my life that I need
to share with You, God. . .**

....

....

....

....

....

....

....

....

THANK YOU, GOD, FOR MAKING ME A
COURAGEOUS GIRL!

**Thank You, God,
for hearing my prayers!
AMEN.**

*This is the day that the Lord has made.
Let us be full of joy and be glad in it.*

PSALM 118:24

Dear God. . .

YOU GIVE ME COURAGE JUST WHEN I NEED IT THE MOST. AND I AM SO THANKFUL! I AM ALSO THANKFUL FOR. . .

You forgive me when I make mistakes—whether they're super small or SUPER BIG. Today, I need Your forgiveness for. . .

I want to shine my light for You, God, so others can see it. And I would like to help build up courage in others too. People I am praying for today. . .

EVEN THOUGH I AM A COURAGEOUS GIRL, I SOMETIMES
WORRY ABOUT THINGS. RIGHT NOW I AM WORRIED ABOUT. . .

....

....

....

AREAS OF MY LIFE WHERE I COULD USE SOME
EXTRA COURAGE INCLUDE. . .

....

....

....

....

....

....

....

....

The life of a courageous girl
is quite busy. Here's what's
going on in my life that I need
to share with You, God. . .

....

....

....

....

....

....

....

THANK YOU, GOD, FOR MAKING ME A
COURAGEOUS GIRL!

Thank You, God,
for hearing my prayers!
AMEN.

*Always give thanks for all things to God the
Father in the name of our Lord Jesus Christ.*

EPHESIANS 5:20

DATE:

Dear God. . . ➤➤

YOU GIVE ME COURAGE JUST WHEN I NEED IT THE MOST. AND I AM SO
THANKFUL! I AM ALSO THANKFUL FOR. . .

You forgive me when I make
mistakes—whether they're super
small or SUPER BIG. Today, I need
Your forgiveness for. . .

I want to shine my light for
You, God, so others can
see it. And I would like to
help build up courage in
others too. People I am
praying for today. . .

EVEN THOUGH I AM A COURAGEOUS GIRL, I SOMETIMES
WORRY ABOUT THINGS. RIGHT NOW I AM WORRIED ABOUT...

AREAS OF MY LIFE WHERE I COULD USE SOME
EXTRA COURAGE INCLUDE...

The life of a courageous girl
is quite busy. Here's what's
going on in my life that I need
to share with You, God. . .

THANK YOU, GOD, FOR MAKING ME A
COURAGEOUS GIRL!

Thank You, God,
for hearing my prayers!
AMEN.

*"Look to the Lord and ask for His strength.
Look to Him all the time."*

1 CHRONICLES 16:11

DATE:

Dear God. . .

YOU GIVE ME COURAGE JUST WHEN I NEED IT THE MOST. AND I AM SO
THANKFUL! I AM ALSO THANKFUL FOR. . .

You forgive me when I make
mistakes—whether they're super
small or SUPER BIG. Today, I need
Your forgiveness for. . .

I want to shine my light for
You, God, so others can
see it. And I would like to
help build up courage in
others too. People I am
praying for today. . .

EVEN THOUGH I AM A COURAGEOUS GIRL, I SOMETIMES WORRY ABOUT THINGS. RIGHT NOW I AM WORRIED ABOUT. . .

....

....

....

....

AREAS OF MY LIFE WHERE I COULD USE SOME EXTRA COURAGE INCLUDE. . .

....

....

....

....

....

....

The life of a courageous girl is quite busy. Here's what's going on in my life that I need to share with You, God. . .

....

....

....

....

....

....

THANK YOU, GOD, FOR MAKING ME A COURAGEOUS GIRL!

Thank You, God, for hearing my prayers! AMEN.

Be holy in every part of your life. Be like the Holy One Who chose you.

1 PETER 1:15

Dear God...

YOU GIVE ME COURAGE JUST WHEN I NEED IT THE MOST. AND I AM SO THANKFUL! I AM ALSO THANKFUL FOR. . .

You forgive me when I make mistakes—whether they're super small or SUPER BIG. Today, I need Your forgiveness for. . .

I want to shine my light for You, God, so others can see it. And I would like to help build up courage in others too. People I am praying for today. . .

EVEN THOUGH I AM A COURAGEOUS GIRL, I SOMETIMES
WORRY ABOUT THINGS. RIGHT NOW I AM WORRIED ABOUT. . .

....

....

....

....

AREAS OF MY LIFE WHERE I COULD USE SOME
EXTRA COURAGE INCLUDE. . .

....

....

....

....

....

....

....

The life of a courageous girl
is quite busy. Here's what's
going on in my life that I need
to share with You, God. . .

....

....

....

....

....

....

....

THANK YOU, GOD, FOR MAKING ME A
COURAGEOUS GIRL!

Thank You, God,
for hearing my prayers!
AMEN.

*And to all these things, you must add love.
Love holds everything and everybody together
and makes all these good things perfect.*

COLOSSIANS 3:14

DATE:

Dear God... »

YOU GIVE ME COURAGE JUST WHEN I NEED IT THE MOST. AND I AM SO THANKFUL! I AM ALSO THANKFUL FOR. . .

You forgive me when I make mistakes—whether they're super small or SUPER BIG. Today, I need Your forgiveness for. . .

I want to shine my light for You, God, so others can see it. And I would like to help build up courage in others too. People I am praying for today. . .

EVEN THOUGH I AM A COURAGEOUS GIRL, I SOMETIMES
WORRY ABOUT THINGS. RIGHT NOW I AM WORRIED ABOUT. . .

....

....

....

AREAS OF MY LIFE WHERE I COULD USE SOME
EXTRA COURAGE INCLUDE. . .

....

....

....

....

....

....

....

The life of a courageous girl
is quite busy. Here's what's
going on in my life that I need
to share with You, God. . .

....

....

....

....

....

....

....

THANK YOU, GOD, FOR MAKING ME A
COURAGEOUS GIRL!

Thank You, God,
for hearing my prayers!
AMEN.

*Say what is good. Your words should
help others grow as Christians.*

EPHESIANS 4:29

Dear God...

YOU GIVE ME COURAGE JUST WHEN I NEED IT THE MOST. AND I AM SO THANKFUL! I AM ALSO THANKFUL FOR. . .

....

....

....

....

You forgive me when I make mistakes—whether they're super small or SUPER BIG. Today, I need Your forgiveness for. . .

I want to shine my light for You, God, so others can see it. And I would like to help build up courage in others too. People I am praying for today. . .

EVEN THOUGH I AM A COURAGEOUS GIRL, I SOMETIMES WORRY ABOUT THINGS. RIGHT NOW I AM WORRIED ABOUT. . .

....
....
....
....

AREAS OF MY LIFE WHERE I COULD USE SOME EXTRA COURAGE INCLUDE. . .

The life of a courageous girl is quite busy. Here's what's going on in my life that I need to share with You, God. . .

....
....
....
....
....
....
....
....

....
....
....
....
....
....
....

THANK YOU, GOD, FOR MAKING ME A COURAGEOUS GIRL!

Thank You, God, for hearing my prayers! AMEN.

You are now children of God because you have put your trust in Christ Jesus.

GALATIANS 3:26

DATE:

Dear God. . .

YOU GIVE ME COURAGE JUST WHEN I NEED IT THE MOST. AND I AM SO THANKFUL! I AM ALSO THANKFUL FOR. . .

You forgive me when I make mistakes—whether they're super small or SUPER BIG. Today, I need Your forgiveness for. . .

I want to shine my light for You, God, so others can see it. And I would like to help build up courage in others too. People I am praying for today. . .

EVEN THOUGH I AM A COURAGEOUS GIRL, I SOMETIMES WORRY ABOUT THINGS. RIGHT NOW I AM WORRIED ABOUT. . .

AREAS OF MY LIFE WHERE I COULD USE SOME EXTRA COURAGE INCLUDE. . .

The life of a courageous girl is quite busy. Here's what's going on in my life that I need to share with You, God. . .

THANK YOU, GOD, FOR MAKING ME A COURAGEOUS GIRL!

Thank You, God, for hearing my prayers! AMEN.

From now on you are not strangers and people who are not citizens. You are citizens together with those who belong to God. You belong in God's family.

EPHESIANS 2:19

DATE:

Dear God. . . **»**

YOU GIVE ME COURAGE JUST WHEN I NEED IT THE MOST. AND I AM SO
THANKFUL! I AM ALSO THANKFUL FOR. . .

....

....

....

....

You forgive me when I make
mistakes—whether they're super
small or SUPER BIG. Today, I need
Your forgiveness for. . .

....

....

....

....

....

....

....

....

....

....

I want to shine my light for
You, God, so others can
see it. And I would like to
help build up courage in
others too. People I am
praying for today. . .

....

....

....

....

....

....

....

....

....

....

....

EVEN THOUGH I AM A COURAGEOUS GIRL, I SOMETIMES
WORRY ABOUT THINGS. RIGHT NOW I AM WORRIED ABOUT. . .

....

....

....

AREAS OF MY LIFE WHERE I COULD USE SOME
EXTRA COURAGE INCLUDE. . .

....

....

....

....

....

....

....

**The life of a courageous girl
is quite busy. Here's what's
going on in my life that I need
to share with You, God. . .**

....

....

....

....

....

THANK YOU, GOD, FOR MAKING ME A
COURAGEOUS GIRL!

**Thank You, God,
for hearing my prayers!
AMEN.**

*For I know that nothing can keep us
from the love of God.*

ROMANS 8:38

MORE IN THE COURAGEOUS GIRLS SERIES!

100 Extraordinary Stories for Courageous Girls

Girls are world-changers! And this deeply inspiring storybook proves it! This collection of 100 extraordinary stories of women of faith—from the Bible, history, and today—will empower you to know and understand how women have made a difference in the world and how much smaller our faith (and the biblical record) would be without them.

Hardback / 978-1-68322-748-9 / $16.99

Cards of Kindness for Courageous Girls: Shareable Devotions and Inspiration

You will delight in spreading kindness and inspiration wherever you go with these shareable *Cards of Kindness*! Each perforated page features a just-right-sized devotional reading plus a positive life message that will both uplift and inspire your young heart.

Paperback / 978-1-64352-164-0 / $7.99

The Bible for Courageous Girls

Part of the exciting "Courageous Girls" book line, this Bible provides complete Old and New Testament text in the easy-reading New Life™ Version, plus insert pages featuring full color illustrations of bold, brave women such as Abigail, Deborah, Esther, Mary Magdalene, and Mary, mother of Jesus.

DiCarta / 978-1-64352-069-8 / $24.99